The 3 Little Pigs And The Power Of A Strong Password
A Cyber Literacy Story

Sandra Estok

Copyright © 2020 by Sandra Estok, MBA, GIAC-GSLC, CIPM – Founder of Way2Protect

Story Adaptation by Elisha Fernández and Sandra Estok

Developmental Editing and Story Strategy by Elayna Fernández

Illustrations by Elisha Fernández

Cover design by SocialClose Media Agency with Illustration by Elisha Fernández

Published by thePositiveMOM.com

All rights reserved.

This book is dedicated to my godchildren.

Elydia and Miguel Angel, you are both my love and inspiration!

Once upon a time, there were 3 little pigs. They lived in 3 different houses on the same street, and they were good friends. One house was made of straw, one of sticks, and the other was made of bricks.

The 3 pigs wanted to buy computers, since they needed to complete homework online. Their moms decided they had reached the appropriate age to have their own devices.

One of the moms found computers on sale online, so she told her neighbors and click, click, click; they purchased their computers.

A week later, 3 identical boxes arrived on each little pig's doorstep. Carefully, they picked up the box, waved to their neighbors, and went inside to set up their brand new laptops.

Little did they know, there was a big, bad, wolf in the neighborhood. He watched them each take a new computer into their home and he grinned maliciously. The big, bad, wolf had been searching for a chance to steal and hack into computers so he could sell it on the big bad wolf market or keep the data for himself and use it later.

Now all he had to do was wait for the perfect opportunity to break in!

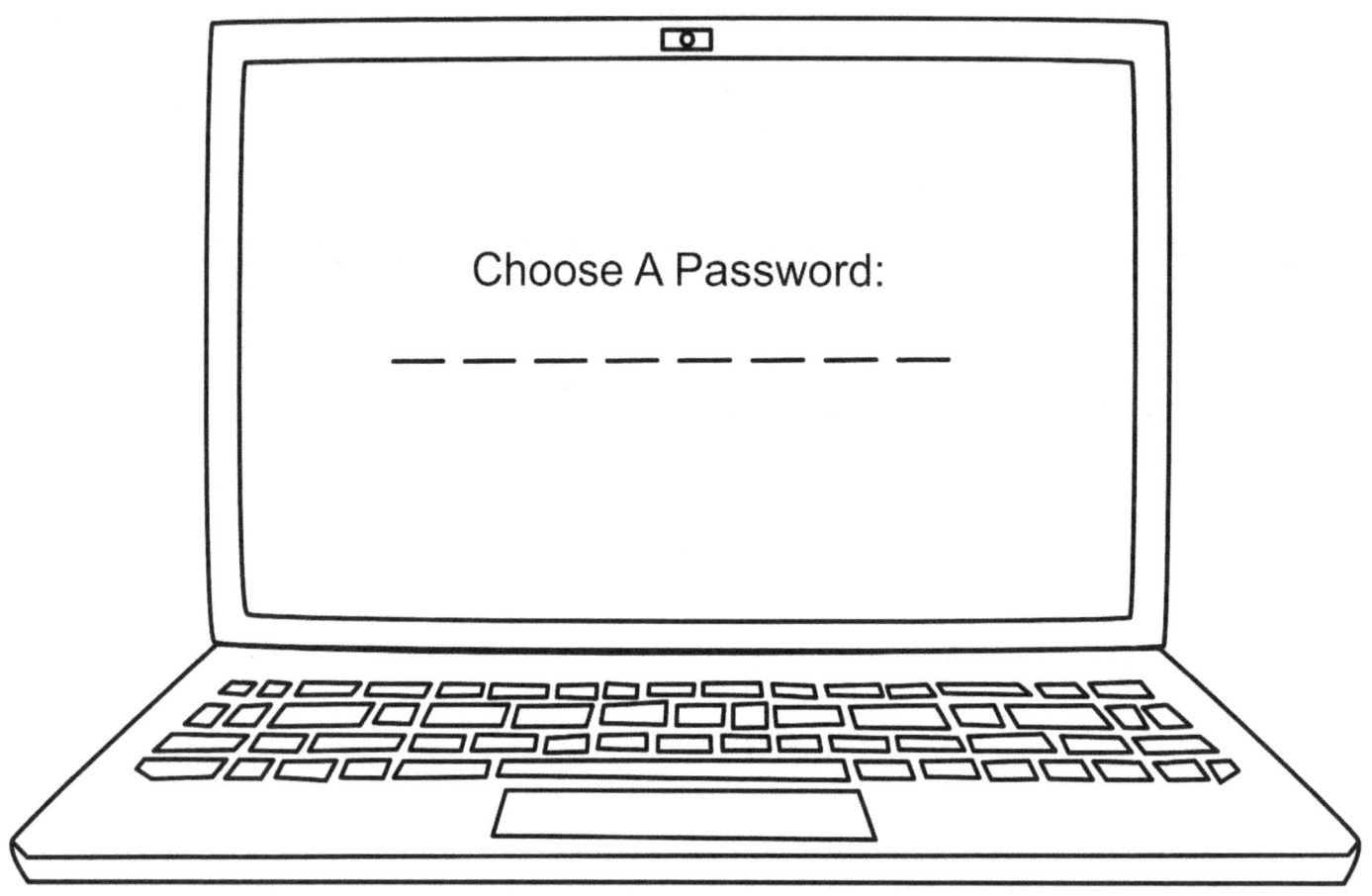

Back to the pigs, they sat in their respective living rooms, admiring the model, size, and shape of their new laptops. Each little pig was excited to begin using their computer.

Their moms helped them set up the computer, but they had one more step in setting up their new device: choosing a password!

The first little pig liked to keep things simple. The system suggested using numbers, special characters and capitalized letters for a strong password.

"There is no way I'm going to remember a password with all these numbers and special characters!" he thought.

The first little pig had very important things to attend to, and decided he simply wouldn't waste time in creating a hard password.

He promptly decided to put the word 'password' as the password to unlock his computer. That way he'd remember it easily. "What a brilliant idea!" he thought. Then the little pig grabbed a jacket, and rushed out the door, leaving it wide open.

At the same time, the second little pig was debating what to use as his password. He had heard horrible stories about hackers stealing data, but he knew that it probably couldn't happen to him because his mom or dad weren't rich or famous. Why would someone want to steal his information?

"I should probably add a number or two in my password, and maybe one capitalized letter. That should be safe enough!" he thought. He typed his password in, and even though the system suggested a stronger password, he ignored the advice and shut his computer.

He wrote his password, '123Password' onto a sticky note, placed it for safekeeping on his desk, and went to play in the backyard.

Meanwhile, the third little pig sat to think. She knew about the dangers surrounding choosing a password that was too simple to guess.

A password would protect her computer and also all her most precious information, her homework, her college funds and where she shares with friends and family online.

She heard that another pig at school had gotten hacked, and all their parents' data and money got stolen. But, she also knew it was hard for her to remember things.

"I want my password to really protect my computer, but also mean something to me so I'll remember it."

She brainstormed the perfect phrase to turn into a password with her mom, since she knew this was valuable time that was worth investing.

After choosing a phrase that made her smile, she remembered that there were some important security tools on her computer that she could activate. If she ever lost her computer, her information would be safe.

After making sure her computer was shut down completely, she placed it on her desk and went to her large bed to take a nice, long nap. She was able to sleep peacefully because she knew her password was protected.

The big, bad wolf knew a lot about the three little pigs. He had been scouting the area and spying on them for weeks now, so he had a good memory of their schedules. He went through their trash and happened to find the boxes: he learned which computers they had bought, and he got ahold of the first two little pigs' names and addresses. The third box had the label removed.

Shortly after pig #1 rushed out of his house in a hurry, the Wolf came to the first front door.

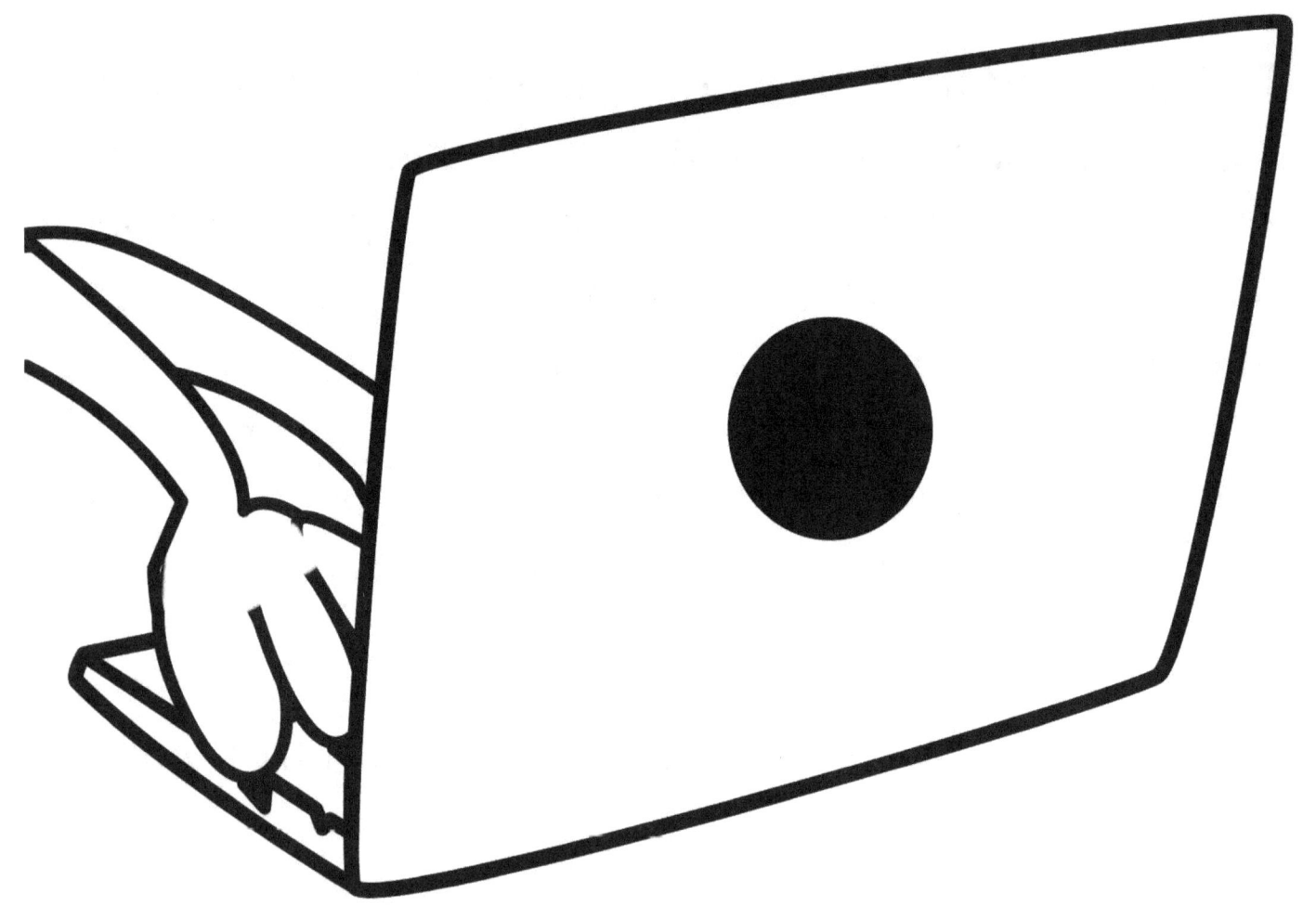

"Little pig, are you home?" he called out, just to be sure. There was no response, and in fact, the door was left open, so he removed some of the straw from the front door, crept in, and there was the computer, sitting on the living room table.

"A-ha!" The wolf grinned cunningly, and tried 'password'. It was the most popular choice for a password, and many people used it.

It worked! He decided to just take the whole computer with him, since it was easy to unlock and free for the taking. He placed it in his bag and started to head out of the door, when something caught his eye.

In her haste, the first little pig's mom had left out several records she had been reviewing earlier: a school report with the names and addresses of all the other moms in the school, medical records, a birth certificate and her credit cards. Thinking all of this would be useful in case he had to make a getaway, he grabbed it and added it to his bag.

Then the wolf headed over to the second house. He noticed it was definitely locked, but there was nothing a little kicking and shoving couldn't solve. After basically breaking down the door, made of fine sticks, he was in.

The noise didn't disturb the second pig, as he had headphones on, listening to music as he was playing in the backyard. It took a bit of searching for the wolf to find the pig's home office, but once he got in, he got on the computer, and tried the same word, 'password'.

It didn't work. "Tsk," the wolf shook his head, this wouldn't be as easy. Then he spotted the sticky note on the desk. He knew that most people write down their passwords to remember them.

Since the second pig was about to come in for a drink of water, the Wolf just took the computer, snatched a USB backup drive that had been carelessly left behind, and a cellphone with no password. This was a big win for the wolf. Feeling proud of himself, he went on his way.

Now it was time to go to the third little pig's house. It was heavily bolted. "Drat!" the wolf whispered to himself. He couldn't break down the door, since it was made of brick. Then he noticed that there were cameras just as he was trying to pick the lock, and the alarm system went off. This little pig was prepared and the wolf would not be able to get in.

The wolf ran out of time, so he decided to come back the next day. He tried to trick the little pig to open the house by pretending to be a friend, but she knew he was not one of his friends. The wolf kept trying to come up with new ways to get in.

"Wait, there are other little pigs that have easier passwords and that don't protect their information," he thought. The wolf decided to find them instead, and left the neighborhood.

Later in the afternoon, the first little pig returned home, he didn't have a computer anymore. He was devastated – all his data was gone! His parents were so angry, too. And "We just spent all this money for nothing," his dad said sadly. His mom was more worried that the access to all his accounts and his identity was in the hands of a complete stranger. They all felt scared and worried.

The second little pig got in to get a drink of water before going back outside. He nearly screamed when he saw the front door in pieces. Now his mom would have to pay extra money to replace the door! His computer was also gone, and he was terrified. He wouldn't be able to complete his homework.

After the third little pig wakes up refreshed from her nap, she realizes they have an alert that her home security had been breached. The third little pig's parents had installed security cameras for her house and they were able to see the face of the big, bad, wolf. She told her parents about the alarm, and they reported it to the local police, who started looking for the wolf, and is able to go on with her day knowing that her data and home are safe.

She decided to talk to her two neighbors, the first and second little pigs, who had their computers stolen by the big, bad, wolf. The parents start talking to each other, and after the third little pig's mom and dad started mentoring the other two families and teaching them how they can be safe and keep their data protected.

They decided to also get brick houses and teach their kids what they could do to do their part and how to create stronger passwords for not only their computers but for all their devices!

And they lived Happily Ever Cyber!

www.ingramcontent.com/pod-product-compliance
Lightning Source LLC
Chambersburg PA
CBHW081758100526
44592CB00015B/2485